M000165744

Earth's crammed with heaven,

And every common bush afire with God;

But only he who sees takes off his shoes —

The rest sit round it and pluck blackberries.

—Elizabeth Barrett Browning

ISBN 0-7683-2666-4

Written by Flavia Weedn
Illustrated by Flavia Weedn
© Weedn Family Trust
All rights reserved.
www.flavia.com

Published in 2003 by Cedco Publishing Company
100 Pelican Way, San Rafael, California 94901
For a free catalog of other Cedco® products, please write
to the address above, or visit our website: www.cedco.com

Manufactured in China

1 3 5 7 9 10 8 6 4 2

No part of this book may be reproduced
in any manner without written permission, except
in the case of reprints in the context of reviews.

A Collection of Poetry

Because of You

Written and Illustrated by
Flavia Weedn

Cedco Publishing · San Rafael, California

Life is painting a picture, not doing a sum.

-Oliver Wendell Holmes

Introduction

I began painting in the 1960s and by the early 1970s I was including within my art the writings of some of the world's most beloved poets. The words spoke directly to my soul and inspired my heart to sing. Though these poets have long since passed from this earth, the feelings they stirred within me stayed very much alive. They were my mentors, my friends, and my colleagues in the romance of life. And the beauty they allowed me to see gave me the courage to begin writing and sharing with the world my own thoughts. My heart fills with gratitude for these wise and loving poets, for it is they who, unknowingly, encouraged me to follow my heart.

This is an overdue letter of thanks. It fulfills a promise I made long ago to these twelve poets who planted within me their seeds of wisdom. Through the years these seeds have been harvested into fields of thought that not only define my work, they define my soul. Though my offering here is humble, I hope they can somehow hear my song of gratitude.

I include brief information about the poets' lives, along with favorite passages. These were gathered from my notes on envelopes, in the margins of sketchbooks, and on scraps of paper found hidden in my purses or coat pockets.

I watched this collection grow through a span of many years, knowing that someday I would have a compilation of work that would hold great meaning for me. I do not claim factual accuracy or correctness in my information, as this book was always personal and intended for me to keep among the things I treasure.

My decision to have this book published now, 30 years after I first compiled it, is a need I feel to share with those who may be unaware of the wonder in these passages which have lain hidden for centuries in old books. As you, the reader, turn these pages of time, it is my sincere hope that you will be able to hear the music I hear.

Flavia

*For Jack, who first introduced me
to these poets when I was a child.
He led me to discover the beauty and
the passion found within
simple drops of ink on paper.
This changed my world.*

Table of Contents

WILLIAM BLAKE
1757-1827

A spiritual, prophetical beauty seemed to surround
Mr. Blake from the year he was born, and continued
throughout his lifetime. It's seen constantly within his work.

> *The Angel that presided o'er my birth*
> *Said, "Little creature, formed of joy and mirth*
> *Go, love without the help of anything on earth."*

It had been predicted that in 1757, the year of his birth, the old
world would end and a new world would begin.

> *To see a World in a grain of sand*
> *And a Heaven in a wild flower,*
> *Hold Infinity in the palm of your hand*
> *And Eternity in an hour.*

When Blake was four, he believed he saw God put his forehead
against the windowpane, and when eight, he was walking in a
field and suddenly saw "a tree filled with angels, and bright
wings covering every branch and bough with stars."

He who binds to himself a Joy
Doth the wing'ed life destroy;
But he who kisses the Joy as it flies
Lives in Eternity's sunrise.

~

The countless gold of a merry heart
The rubies and pearls of a loving eye,
The indolent never can bring to the mart,
Nor the secret hoard up in his treasury.

With no formal schooling, he began engraving as a child.
How incredible that he had the persistence and courage to
accomplish all that he did during his lifetime, and to leave such
great inspiration for future generations.

How sweet I roam'd from field to field
And tasted all of summer's pride,
Till I the prince of love beheld
Who in the sunny beams did glide.

~

He loves to sit and hear me sing,
Then, laughing, sports and plays with me;
Then stretches out my golden wing,
And mocks my loss of liberty.

Between the ages of twelve and twenty, Mr. Blake wrote poems
that were as beautiful as anything ever written in all of
English literature.

Piping down the valleys wild,
Piping songs of pleasant glee,
On a cloud I saw a child,
And he, laughing said to me:

'Pipe a song about a lamb!'
So I piped with merry cheer.
'Piper, pipe that song again.'
So I piped; he wept to hear.

'Drop thy pipe, thy happy pipe;
Sing thy songs of happy cheer!
So I sang the same again,
While he wept with joy to hear.

'Piper, sit thee down and write
In a book, that all may read.'
So he vanished from my sight,
And I plucked a hollow reed,

And I made a rural pen,
And I stained the water clear,
And I wrote my happy songs
Every child may joy to hear.

In his twenties, he married a girl who had a natural talent for drawing. She became Blake's wife and his partner.

Love seeketh not itself to please,
Nor for itself hath any care,
But for another gives its ease,
And builds a Heaven in Hell's despair.

Together they presented his *Songs of Innocence* in the most unusual way known to printing at the time. The poems were not printed, but drawn in varnish onto metal plates, then dipped into acid. The part that was left after the acid bath stood out like engravings.

Man was made for Joy and Woe;
And when this we rightly know,
Thro' the World we safely go,
Joy and Woe are woven fine,
A Clothing for the Soul divine.
Under every grief and pine
Runs a joy with silken twine.

~

The moon like a flower
In heaven's high bower,
With silent delight
Sits and smiles on the night.

~

Tyger! Tyger! burning bright
In the forests of the night,
What immortal hand or eye
Could frame thy fearful symmetry?

~

No bird soars too high if he soars with his own wings.

Mr. Blake and his wife worked long and hard hours to present his books, which were so unlike any other poet's works. He wrote, engraved, and illustrated a series of prophetic books both

in verse and prose. The couple supported themselves by the sale
of his books. He also created illustrations for other writers.

One Mite wrung from the Lab'rer's hands
Shall buy and sell the Miser's Lands;
Or, if protected from on high,
Does that whole Nation sell and buy.

His works seem to represent the feelings of the human spirit,
as if he saw and felt everything, not with logic but with
his imagination.

Does the Eagle know what is in the pit?
Or wilt thou go ask the Mole?
Can Wisdom be put in a silver rod?
Or Love in a golden bowl?

There is a mystic, childlike wonder to everything Blake writes,
unlike the feeling of maturity and reality with which most
poets write. To him, innocence has its own wisdom. It is no
wonder that his wife often stated she had very little of Mr.
Blake's company, for he was always in "Paradise."

When the voices of children are heard on the green,
And laughing is heard on the hill,
My heart is at rest within my breast
And everything else is still.

~

Memory, higher come, and tune your merry notes;
And, while upon the wind your music floats,
I'll pour upon the stream where sighing lovers dream,
And fish for fancies as they pass within the watery glass.

~

If you trap the moment before it's ripe,
The tears of repentance you'll certainly wipe;
But if once you let the ripe moment go
You can never wipe off the tears of woe.

~

Never seek to tell thy love
Love that never told can be;
For the gentle wind does move
Silently, invisibly.

He lived the last years of his life in poverty, unrecognized by his contemporaries, and yet he continued to write and express the revelations of his creative and mystic mind until he died.

Great things are done when men and mountains meet.

Dear Mr. Blake, you have helped me see a new world, one I thought existed only in my mind. I close with one line, which, to me, you wrote as though you wished to share a secret.

And I give you the end of a golden string …

WILLIAM WORDSWORTH
1770—1850

$\mathcal{M}$r. Wordsworth was orphaned when he was eight. He and his other four siblings were scattered among schools and guardians. At seventeen he began to write, and even then his work expressed his appreciation for simply being alive.

Bliss was it in that dawn to be alive,
But to be young was very heaven!

~

Thou, whose exterior semblance doth belie
Thy soul's immensity ....

~

I wandered lonely as a cloud
That floats on high o'er vales and hills,
When all at once I saw a crowd,
A host of golden daffodils,
Beside the lake, beneath the trees
Fluttering and dancing in the breeze.

Ten thousand saw I at a glance,
Tossing their heads in sprightly dance.

A poet could not but be gay,
In such a jocund company:
I gazed — and gazed — but little thought
What wealth the show to me had brought.

~

She lived unknown, and few could know
When Lucy ceased to be;
But she is in her grave, and oh,
The difference to me!

Thou hast left behind
Powers that will work for thee; air, earth and skies;
There's not a breathing of the common wind
That will forget thee; thou hast great allies;
Thy friends are exultations, agonies,
And love, and man's unconquerable mind.

~

Ah, little doth the young-one dream,
When full of play and childish cares,
What power is in his wildest scream,
Heard by his mother unawares!
He knows it not, he cannot guess;
Years to a mother bring distress;
But do not make her love the less.

~

Come forth into the light of things,
Let Nature be your teacher.

When Mr. Wordsworth was in his twenties, he fell deeply in love with a girl and fathered a child. Their marriage plans were made, only to be postponed. This was a very sad time for him when it should have been a joyous one, and could have been, except for the condition of the world and its effect upon him.

There was a time when meadow, grove, and stream,
The earth, and every common sight,
To me did seem
Appareled in celestial light,
The glory and the freshness of a dream.

It is now as it hath been of yore;
Turn whereso'er I may,
By night or day,
The things which I have seen I now can see no more.

~

The stars of midnight shall be dear
To her; and she shall lean her ear
In many a secret place
Where rivulets dance their wayward round,
And beauty born of murmuring sound
Shall pass into her face.

At this time much unrest was in Europe, and France and England were fighting a war. Because of this, both the planning of his life and the marriage to his French sweetheart were postponed time and time again, and never came to pass.

Men are we, and must grieve when even the shade
Of that which once was great, is passed away.

~

The sunshine is a glorious birth;
But yet I know, where'er I go,
That there hath passed away
A glory from the earth.

~

To her fair works did Nature link
The human soul that through me ran;
And much it grieved my heart to think
What man has made of man.

Yet ten years later, he, his daughter and her mother walked along the beach near Calais. In that time and place, some of his most beautiful sonnets were written.

But hearing oftentimes
The still, sad music of humanity …

~

A violet by a mossy stone
Half hidden from the eye.
Fair as a star, when only one
Is shining in the sky.

~

Yet sometimes, when the secret cup
Of still and serious thought went round,

It seemed as if he drank it up —
He felt with spirit so profound.

~

She gave me eyes, she gave me ears;
And humble cares, and delicate fears;
A heart, the fountain of sweet tears;
And love, and thought, and joy.

~

The music in my heart I bore
Long after it was heard no more.

~

Though nothing can bring back the hour
Of splendour in the grass, of glory in the flower;
We will grieve not, rather find
Strength in what remains behind;
In the primal sympathy
Which having been must ever be;
In the soothing thoughts that spring
Out of human suffering;
In the faith that looks through death
In years that bring the philosophic mind.

~

Where is it now, the glory of the dream?

~

All things that love the sun are out of doors;
The sky rejoices in the morning's birth;
The grass is bright with rain-drops ... on the moors
The hare is running races in her mirth;

And with her feet she from the plashy earth
Raises a mist, that glittering in the sun,
Runs with her all the way, wherever she doth run.

Later Mr. Wordsworth spent much time with his sister and lived with her in England. She and her love for "common things" heavily influenced him.

Knowing that Nature never did betray
The heart that loved her.

~

Sensations sweet,
Felt in the blood, and felt along the heart.

~

A slumber did my spirit seal;
I had no human fears;
She seemed a thing that could not feel
The touch of earthly years.

Samuel Coleridge became his close friend and he and Mr. Wordsworth's sister worked and wrote together daily, and later became engaged.

What if the rose-streak of morning
Pale and depart in a passion of tears?
Once to have hoped is no matter for scorning!
Love once ... e'en love's disappointment endears!

~

Often have I sighed to measure by myself a lonely pleasure,
Sighed to think, I read a book only read, perhaps by me.

~

That best portion of a good man's life —
His little, nameless, unremembered acts
Of kindness and of love.

~

There's not a man that lives
That hath not known his god-like hours.

His definition of poetry is reflected in his work, for poem after poem reveal his recollections of beloved sights and times, and emotional feelings of the heart.

I have said that poetry is the spontaneous overflow of powerful
feelings: it takes its origin from emotion recollected in tranquility.

~

O Reader! had you in your mind
Such stores as silent thought can bring,
O gentle Reader! you would find a tale in everything.

~

My heart leaps up when I behold a rainbow in the sky;
So it was when my life began;
So is it now I am a man;
So be it when I shall grow old, or let me die.

~

Earth fills her lap with pleasures of her own ...

~

A sense sublime
Of something far more deeply interfused,
Whose dwelling is the light of setting suns,
And the round ocean and the living air,
And the blue sky, and in the mind of man;
A motion and a spirit, that impels
All thinking things, all objects of all thought
And rolls through all things.

~

I've wet my path with tears like dew,
weeping for him when no one knew.

(following Coleridge's death)

~

Can we love but on condition
that the thing we love must die?

~

And 'tis my faith that every flower enjoys the air it breathes.

~

Thanks to the human heart by which we live,
Thanks to its tenderness, its joys, and fears,
To me the meanest flower that blows can give
Thoughts that do often lie too deep for tears.

Mr. Wordsworth was a true romantic, disliked artificial things, and loved simplicity. His work was touched with philosophy and I was drawn to that. Perhaps this is why I used his words in my earlier paintings more than those of any other poet. Often I wondered if he thought his writings would touch anyone as they have me, these more than a hundred years later. Then I discovered the following two lines:

Enough if something from our hands have power
To live, and act, and serve the future hour.

~

The soft blue sky did never melt
Into his heart; he never felt
The witchery of the soft blue sky!

~

Sweet childish days, that were as long as twenty days are now.

~

The daisy, by the shadow that it casts,
Protects the lingering dewdrop from the sun.

~

A youth to whom was given ...
So much of earth ... so much of heaven.

~

How does the meadow-flower its bloom unfold?
Because the lovely little flower is free
Down to its root, and, in that freedom, bold.

~

Now, for that consecrated fount
Of murmuring, sparkling, living love,

What have I? Shall I dare to tell?
A well of love ... it may be deep ...
I trust it is ... and never dry;
What matter? If the waters sleep
In silence and obscurity.
Such change, and at the very door
Of my fond heart, hath made me poor.

~

Such a starved bank of moss
Till that May-morn,
Blue ran the flash across;
Violets were born!

I close this chapter, Mr. Wordsworth, with the following, one
of my most favorite stanzas.

Scorn not the Sonnet; critic, you have frowned,
Mindless of its just honours; with this key
Shakespeare unlocked his heart.

THOMAS MOORE
1779-1852

*M*r. Moore was born in Dublin, of Irish parents. He achieved prominence not only for his poetry, but for his patriotism and great personal charm.

> *And the heart that is soonest awake to the flowers*
> *Is always the first to be touched by the thorns.*

> *To sigh, yet feel no pain;*
> *To weep, yet scarce know why;*
> *To sport an hour with Beauty's chain,*
> *Then throw it idly by.*

> *Humility, that low, sweet root*
> *From which all heavenly virtues shoot.*

> *Give smiles to those who love you less,*
> *But keep your tears for me.*

> *No eye to watch, and no tongue to wound us,*
> *All earth forgot, and all heaven around us.*

Alas! How light a cause may move dissension between hearts that love.

He is remembered largely for his *Irish Melodies*, a group of songs published between 1808 and 1834.

But there's nothing half so sweet in life
As love's young dream.

Ah! little they think who delight in her strains,
How the heart of the Minstrel is breaking.

Go where glory waits thee!
But while fame elates thee,
Oh, still remember me!

And when once the young heart of a maiden is stolen,
The maiden herself will steal after it soon.

You may break, you may shatter the vase if you will,
But the scent of the roses will hang round it still.

His *Irish Melodies* were later set to music. Some became classics through the years and have kept lasting fame.

Believe me, if all those endearing young charms
Which I gaze on so fondly today,
Were to change by tomorrow and fleet in my arms,
Like fairy gifts fading away.
Thou would'st still be adored as this moment thou art,
Let thy loveliness fade as it will.
And around the dear ruin each wish of my heart
Would entwine itself verdantly still.

Oft in the stilly night,
Ere slumber's chain has bound me,
Fond memory brings the light
Of other days around me;
The smiles, the tears, of boyhood's years,
The words of love then spoken;
The eyes that shone now dimmed and gone,
The cheerful hearts now broken.

He wrote many satires, and his poem "Lalla Rookh," written in 1817, was considered one of the most popular poems of his day. His close friend was Lord Byron, who willed him his memoirs. He wrote Lord Byron's biography in 1830 and this was recognized as one of his best prose works.

As down in the sunless retreats of the ocean
Sweet flowers are springing no mortal can see,
So, deep in my soul the still prayer of devotion,
Unheard by the world, rises silent to Thee.

Within his work, I found a simplicity of word and loving touch
that combines his gentleness with his deep faith.

Oh, call it by some better name, for friendship sounds so cold.

But Faith, fanatic Faith, once wedded fast
To some dear falsehood, hugs it to the last.

And the tear that we shed, though in secret it rolls,
Shall long keep his memory green in our souls.

So Life's year begins and closes;
Days though shortening still can shine;
What through youth gave love and roses
Age still leaves us friends and wine.

Oh! ever thus, from childhood's hour,
I've seen my fondest hope decay;
I never loved a tree or flower,
But 'twas the first to fade away.
I never nurs'd a dear gazelle
To glad me with its soft black eye,
But when it came to know me well
And love me it was sure to die.

Came but from Friendship, and took away Love.

And so, dear Mr. Moore, I come to the end of your chapter.
I humbly offer my gratitude to you for sharing with the world
the beauty found in the expression of your thoughts.

No, the heart that has truly lov'd never forgets,
But as truly loves on to the close,
As the sunflower turns on her god, when he sets,
The same look which she turn'd when he rose.

Shall I ask the brave soldier, who fights by my side
In the cause of mankind, if our creeds agree?
Shall I give up the friend I have valued and tried,
If he kneel not before the same altar with me?

JOHN KEATS
1795-1821

*M*r. Keats came from quite a different background than most other poets I write about here. He was born the son of a stable hand who cleaned the stalls in his grandfather's livery stable.

> *I stood tip-toe upon a little hill,*
> *The air was cooling, and so very still.*
> *And then there crept*
> *A little noiseless noise among the leaves,*
> *Born of the very sigh that silence heaves.*
>
> ~
>
> *Open a fresh round of starry folds,*
> *Ye ardent marigolds!*

When he was only ten his father was killed, so he grew up with his mother and grandmother. In school he was known as a fighter, which was probably the result of his insecurity due to his slight build. He studied medicine intermittently, but the turning point in his life came when he was given Chapman's translation of Homer. The first night he read it, he was so completely excited with its discovery that he stayed up all night working on what was to become one of his most famous

sonnets, "On First Looking Into Chapman's Homer." He
began to develop a deep sensitivity to words, and seemed to live
in a world of dreams.

A bright torch, and a casement ope at night,
To let the warm Love in!

~

Life is but a day;
A fragile dew drop on its perilous way
From a tree's summit.

~

The poetry of earth is never dead.

~

E'en like the passage of an angel's tear
That falls through the clear ether silently.

~

There is an awful warmth about my heart
like a load of immortality.

~

To sorrow,
I bade good-morrow,
And thought to leave her far away behind;
But cheerly, cheerly,
She loves me dearly;
She is so constant to me, and so kind.

~

When I behold, upon the night's starr'd face,
Huge cloudy symbols of a high romance.

He was licensed to practice medicine but never did; instead he became entirely involved with his writings, all of which seem to be filled with imagination and beauty.

Asleep in lap of legends old.

~

Too many tears for lovers have been shed,
Too many sighs give we to them in fee,
Too much doleful stories do we see,
Whose matter in bright gold were best be read.

~

Blue! Gentle cousin of the forest-green,
Married to green in all the sweetest flowers, —
Forget me not, — the blue bell, — and that Queen
Of Secrecy, the violet.

~

If poetry comes not naturally as leaves to a tree
It had better not come at all.

~

Shed no tear … O shed no tear!
The flower will bloom another year.
Weep no more … O weep no more,
Young buds sleep in the root's white core.

When Mr. Keats was twenty-one, he became involved in a literary circle for the first time. He met Mr. Wordsworth, Mr. Shelley, and Mr. Coleridge, but only with Mr. Leigh Hunt, who became his sponsor, did he become close friends.

Wherein lies happiness? In that which becks
Our ready minds to fellowship divine,
A fellowship with essence; 'till we shine,
Full alchemiz'd, and free of space. Behold
The clear religion of heaven!

The crown of these
Is made of love and friendship, and sits high
Upon the forehead of humanity.

Mr. Keats became ill for a time, and went to the countryside because of his illness.

To one who has been long in city pent,
'Tis very sweet to look into the fair
And open face of heaven.

~

But strength alone though of the Muses born
Is like a fallen angel: trees uptorn,
Darkness, and worms, and shrouds, and sepulchers
Delight it; for it feeds upon the burrs
And thorns of life; forgetting the great end
Of poesy, that it should be a friend
To soothe the cares, and lift the thoughts of man.

~

And they are gone; aye, ages long ago
These lovers fled away into the storm.

When Mr. Keats later returned to London, he found that he and his work had been severely criticized in two important literary publications.

I am certain of nothing but the holiness of the heart's affections
and the truth of imagination — what the imagination seizes as
beauty must be truth — whether it existed before or not.

~

"Beauty is truth, truth beauty" — that is all
Ye know on earth, and all ye need to know.

The publications had made fun of his humble beginnings, and he was deeply hurt. Many of his close friends believed the attacks helped to hasten his death.

Sudden a thought came like a full-blown rose,
Flushing his brow, and in his pained heart
Made purple riot.

~

Pleasure is oft a visitant; but pain clings cruelly to us.

~

There is not a fiercer hell than the failure in a great object.

Just before he died, while still very ill, he had a deep but unhappy love affair. During this sad time in his short life, he wrote the poems that he is most remembered for.

Bright star, were I as steadfast as thou art —
Not in lone splendour hung aloft the night
And watching, with eternal lids apart,
Like nature's patient, sleepless Eremite.
The moving waters at their priestlike task
Of pure ablution round earth's human shores.

~

Already with thee! Tender is the night.

Mr. Keats, your poems are often filled with the details of your own sense of sad ecstasy. This show of your sensitive emotion and the richness of your work is one of the reasons I am drawn to you. You make me realize that I already have begun to bare my soul to the world, and that I also see this same sense of sad ecstasy in life.

Was it a vision, or a waking dream?
Fled is that music: — Do I wake or sleep?

~

Heard melodies are sweet, but those unheard are sweeter.

~

Forever wilt thou love, and she be fair!

~

I cannot see what flowers are at my feet,
Nor what soft incense hangs upon the boughs,
But in embalmed darkness, guess each sweet.

Dear Mr. Keats, I close your chapter with some of your most beautiful and remembered words. And I thank you.

> *A thing of beauty is a joy forever:*
> *Its loveliness increases; it will never*
> *Pass into nothingness; but still will keep*
> *A bower quiet for us, and a sleep*
> *Full of sweet dreams, and health, and quiet breathing.*

Percy Bysshe Shelley
1792-1822

*M*r. Shelley was English. As a child he was brilliant but extremely sensitive, and because of this his schooling was miserable for him. His peers did not accept him and this continued even while he attended Oxford, from which he was expelled at nineteen for publishing anonymously, *The Necessity of Atheism*. He then eloped with a seventeen-year–old girl.

> *A lovely lady, garmented in light,*
> *From her own beauty.*

Together they became very involved politically. He and his wife distributed papers called *Declaration of Rights*, putting some in bottles, sending some up in balloons. He seemed to be caught up in youth's desire to better an existing world. He became very adamant about his feelings and expressed them in his poems; he was becoming a greet seeker of truth.

> *Death is the veil which those who live call life:*
> *They sleep, and it is lifted.*

~

Make me thy lyre, even as the forest is:
What if my leaves are falling like its own!
The tumult of thy mighty harmonies
Will take from both a deep, autumnal tone,
Sweet though in sadness. Be thou, Spirit fierce.
My spirit! Be thou me, impetuous one!

~

That orbed maiden with white fire laden,
Whom mortals call the moon.

~

The awful shadow of some unseen Power
floats though unseen, among us — visiting
This various world with as inconstant wing
As summer winds that creep from flower to flower.

~

All the earth and air with thy voice is loud.
As, when night is bare, from one lonely cloud
The moon rains out her beams, and heaven is overflowed.

His first poem was published after he became a father at twenty-one, and within the next few years he had many love affairs, before moving to Italy. There, away from Britain, he became more devoted to expressing his ideals, rather than his politics, in his poetry.

I arise from dreams of thee
In the first sweet sleep of night,
When the winds are breathing low,
And the stars are shining bright.

~

I could lie down like a tired child,
And weep away the life of care
Which I have borne and yet must bear ...

His personal life was marked by tragedy and drama. Women committed suicide over him; he had two children by two women — both of whom shared the same father. He seemed to become much too emotionally entangled, and perhaps this was due to his intense capacity for love and his deep sensitivity.

It is our will
That thus enchains us to permitted ill ...
We might be otherwise ... we might be all
We dream of happy, high majestical.
Where is the love, beauty and truth we seek
But in our mind?

~

Teas—where small talk dies in agonies.

~

Thou art unseen, — but yet I hear thy shrill delight.

~

We look before and after,
And pine for what is not;
But sincerest laughter
With some pain is fraught;
Our sweetest songs are those
That tell of saddest thought.

~

He is a portion of the loveliness
Which once he made more lovely.

~

I love Love — though he has wings,
And like light can flee,
But above all other things,
Spirit, I love thee —
Thou art love and life! O come!
Make once more my heart thy home!

Aside from his loves and personal life, for a while he seemed to want to reform the world. Later, he seemed to do a turnabout and rebelled against himself.

Hail to thee, blithe Spirit!
Bird thou never wert,
That from Heaven, or near it,
Pourest thy full heart
In profuse strains of unpremeditated art.

~

In the golden lightning of the sunken sun
O'er which clouds are bright'ning
Thou dost float and run,
Like an unbodied joy whose race is just begun.

His rebellion was apparent as he wrote his revolutionary poems. At the same time, he could cast almost a hypnotic spell over his readers with a gentleness of spirit.

Like stars half quencht in mists of silver dew.

~

O Wind,
If winter comes, can spring be far behind?

~

All love is sweet,
Given or returned. Common as light is love,
And its familiar voice wearies not ever ...
They who inspire it most are fortunate,
As I am now; but those who feel it most
Are happier still.

~

A sensitive Plant in a garden grew
And the young winds fed it with silver Dew.

~

I love all waste
And solitary places; where we taste
The pleasure of believing what we see
Is boundless, as we wish our souls to be.

~

Music, when soft voices die,
Vibrates in the memory;
Odours, when sweet violets sicken,
Live within the sense they quicken.

Sadly, during his lifetime Mr. Shelley was rarely thought of as a good poet. He knew this, and had a sadness in much of his poems, as if he were crying out his grief to the world — not just for himself but for all rejected poets.

For love and beauty and delight,
There is no death nor change.

~

Silver key of the fountain of tears,
Where the spirit drinks till the brain is wild;
Softest grave of a thousand fears,
Where their mother, Care, like a drowsy child
Is laid asleep in flowers.

~

I am the daughter of Earth and Water,
And the nursling of the Sky;
I pass through the pores of the ocean and shores,
I change, but I cannot die.

~

The seed ye sow, another reaps;
The wealth ye find, another keeps;
The robes ye weave, another wears;
The arms ye forge, another bears.

While sailing in a storm off Italy, Mr. Shelley drowned at age twenty-nine, leaving unfinished his last and maybe his greatest visionary poem, "The Triumph of Life." Mr. Shelley's work as a whole represents one of the most sublime spirits the world has ever known, and yet his first edition of collected poems wasn't published until 1839, seventeen years after his death.

Spirit of Beauty, that dost consecrate
With thine own hues all thou dost shine upon
Of human thought or form.

~

Nothing in the world is single,
All things by a law divine
In one spirit meet and mingle.
Why not I with thine?

~

And one with trembling hands clasps his cold head,
And fans him with her moonlight wings, and cries,
'Our love, our hope, our sorrow, is not dead;
See, on the silken fringe of his faint eyes,
Like dew upon a sleeping flower, there lies
A tear some Dream has loosened from his brain.'

~

Lost Angel of a ruined Paradise!
She knew not 'twas her own; as with no stain
She faded, like a cloud which had outwept the rain.

(following the death of John Keats)

~

Sing again, with your dear voice revealing a tone
Of some world far from ours,
Where music and moonlight and feeling are one.

What thou art we know not;
What is most like thee?
From rainbow clouds there flow not
Drops so bright to see
As from thy presence showers a rain of melody.

~

Sound of vernal showers
On the twinkling grass,
Rain-awakened flowers,
All that ever was
Joyous and clear, and fresh,
Thy music doth surpass.

~

Heaven's ebon vault,
Studded with stars unutterably bright,
Through which the moon's unclouded grandeur rolls,
Seems like a canopy which love had spread
To curtain her sleeping world.

~

I bring fresh showers for the thirsting flowers,
From the seas and the streams.
I bear light shade for the leaves when laid
In their noonday dreams.

Your life, Mr. Shelley, seemed to be the most colorful and
lyrical, yet the saddest of any of the poets' in this collection.
With your loves, marriages, wealth, loss of wealth, despairs and

tragedies, you left the world some of the most beautiful poems ever written. Who can tell how many others became poets because of your influence. I am deeply touched by the beauty and sensitivity of spirit in your work, and I thank you for letting me listen.

Yet if we could scorn
Hate, and pride, and fear;
If we were things born
Not to shed a tear,
I know not how thy joy
We ever should come near.

~

Teach me half the gladness
That thy brain must know,
Such harmonious madness
From my lips would flow
The world would listen then,
As I am listening now.

RALPH WALDO EMERSON
1803-1882

*M*r. Emerson was born the son of a minister in Boston, Massachusetts. It was planned from his childhood that he would become a minister like his father. He was ordained when he was twenty-six, but left the ministry three years later.

Nothing can bring you peace but yourself.

Nature is a mutable cloud, which is always and never the same.

Solitude, the safeguard of mediocrity, is to genius, the stern friend.

At twenty-nine, he was married, began a new life, and was becoming known as an educator as well as a chaplain.

Great men are they who see that the spiritual is stronger than any material force; that thoughts rule the world.

A man is a bundle of relations, a knot of roots,
whose flower and fruitage is the world.

~

Make yourself necessary to somebody.

~

Shallow men believe in luck.

~

Hitch your wagon to a star.

Tragedy struck Mr. Emerson three years after his marriage, when his wife died of tuberculosis, as had his father and two brothers. He then journeyed abroad, met and became friends with Mr. Coleridge and Mr. Carlyle, and later returned to Massachusetts. He remarried and began a life of lecturing, during which time he published his first volume of work, called *Nature*.

Everything in Nature contains all the powers of Nature.
Everything is made of one hidden stuff.

~

He is great who is what he is from Nature,
And who never reminds us of others.

Poems and essays began to flow from him ... most of them stating that man was being dominated by things rather than by thoughts.

What is a weed?
A plant whose virtues have not yet been discovered.

If eyes were made for seeing,
Then beauty is its own excuse for being.

Nature and books belong to the eyes that see them.

Thou art to me a delicious torment.

A friend is a person with whom I may be sincere.
Before him, I may think aloud.

During this time, Harvard began to resent Mr. Emerson and would no longer let him lecture, due to his political views.

I wish to write such rhymes as shall not suggest a restraint, but
contrariwise the wildest freedom.

Men grind and grind in the mill of a truism,
and nothing comes out but what was put in.
But the moment they desert the tradition for
a spontaneous thought, then poetry, wit, hope, virtue, learning,
anecdote all flock to their aid.

Life is too short to waste
in critic peep or cynic bark,
Quarrel or reprimand.

'Twill soon be dark;
Up! Mind thine own aim, and
God speed the mark.

~

I hate quotation. Tell me what you know.

~

For everything you have missed, you have gained something else;
and for everything you gain, you lose something.

Ironically, thirty years later he received an honorary degree from Harvard, and at sixty-seven, he taught a course at Cambridge on philosophy.

The only gift is a portion of thyself.

~

It is as impossible for a man to be cheated by any one
but himself, as for a thing to be,
And not to be, at the same time.

When Mr. Emerson was seventy years old, he lost all the books and other things he had loved and collected when his house burned and was completely destroyed. His friends insisted he journey abroad, and while he was gone they rebuilt the house in every detail.

A friend may well be reckoned the masterpiece of Nature.

The reward of a thing well done, is to have done it.

When he returned, he went into seclusion with his energy and his memory rapidly fading.

> *It is time to be old,*
> *To take in sail.*

This unusually talented man had his work appear conventional on the surface, like so many poets. But it was deceptive because his ideas, which were considered radical for that time, show through in some of his work.

> *Oh, tenderly, the haughty dog*
> *Fills his blue urn with fire.*

> *Things are in the saddle,*
> *And ride mankind.*

> *The world uncertain comes and goes,*
> *The lover rooted stays.*

> *Do not say things. What you are stands over you the while,*
> *and thunders so that I cannot hear*
> *what you say to the contrary.*

These statements show Emerson, the man, both truth-loving and life-loving. Those like myself, who enjoy his work, do so because we can actually touch and hold on to his feelings for a moment.

All mankind loves a lover.

Art is a jealous mistress, and if a man have a genius of painting,
poetry, music, architecture, or philosophy,
he makes a bad husband, and an ill provider.

I wiped away the weeds and foam,
I fetched my sea-born treasures home;
But the poor, unsightly, noisome things
Had left their beauty on the shore,
With the sun and the sand and the wild uproar.

Give me health and a day, and I will make the pomp
of emperors ridiculous.

There are two classes of poets ... the poets by education
and practice, these we respect;
And poets by nature, these we love ...

There is no beautifier of complexion, or form, or behaviour, like
the wish to scatter joy and not pain around us.

Elizabeth Barrett Browning
1806-1861

*T*his brief sketch of the life of Elizabeth Barrett Browning could be a fairy tale because of its story of love. She was thirty-nine years old and an invalid, living with a domineering and possessive father, when she first met Robert Browning.

> *How many desolate creatures on the earth*
> *Have learnt the simple dues of fellowship*
> *And social comfort in a hospital.*
>
> ~
>
> *The beautiful seems right*
> *By force of Beauty, and the feeble wrong*
> *Because of Weakness.*

Their romance began with correspondence and grew into secret visits.

> *A little sunburnt by the glare of life.*
>
> ~
>
> *Every wish is like a prayer, with God.*

These visits grew into more visits and then deepened into love, and in 1846 they eloped.

Men do not think
Of sons and daughters, when they fall in love.

They left for Italy and lived there. He wrote of his love for her so often before they married, and it was returned countless times in many of her poems expressing her love for him following their marriage.

I should not dare to call my soul my own.

~

When our two souls stand up erect and strong,
Face to face, silent, drawing nigh and nigher.

~

How do I love thee? Let me count the ways
I love thee to the depth and breadth and height
My soul can reach, when feeling out of sight
For the ends of Being and ideal Grace.
I love thee to the level of every day's
Most quiet need, by sun and candle-light.
I love thee freely, as men strive for right;
I love thee with the passion put to use
In my old griefs, and with my childhood's faith.
I love thee with a love I seemed to lose
With my lost saints ... I love thee with the breath,
Smiles, tears, of all my life! — and if God choose,
I shall but love thee better after death.

And I smiled to think God's greatness
flowed around our incompleteness;
Round our restlessness, His rest.

If thou must love me, let it be for naught
except for love's sake only.

The wildest land
Doom takes to part us, leaves thy heart in mine
With pulses that beat double. What I do
And what I dream include thee, as the wine
Must taste of its own grapes. And when I sue
God for myself, He hears that name of thine
And sees within my eyes, the tears of two.

At first her poems were not meant for publication, they were simply tributes to him. In the 1800s, some critics of literature felt that her work was lacking and her eminence had declined. How sad, for at one time, her sonnet, "How Do I Love Thee?" was considered one of the greatest love poems ever written.

God only, who made us rich, can make us poor.

Her father had never forgiven her for leaving him, and did not hide how he felt from the rest of the world. Publicly he stated openly that their marriage was cursed from the beginning and would never last.

Earth's crammed with heaven,
And every common bush afire with God;
But only he who sees takes off his shoes —
The rest sit round it and pluck blackberries.

How wrong her father was. Not only did their love grow, but her health improved enough for her to give birth to a son when she was forty-four.

Do you hear the children weeping,
O my brothers.
Ere the sorrow comes with years?

The child's sob in the silence curses deeper
Than the strong man in his wrath.

She died in her husband's arms after fifteen years of a love-filled storybook marriage. Her death ended one of the most beautiful real-life love stories to be born in literature.

We walked too straight for fortune's end,
We loved too true to keep a friend.
At last we're tired, my heart and I.

~

Of all the thoughts of God that are
Borne inward into souls afar,
Along the Psalmist's music deep,
Now tell me if that any is,
For gift or grace, surpassing this;
'He giveth his beloved ... sleep.'

My dear Mrs. Browning, I end this chapter as a tribute to you, with one of my favorite verses. Thank you for sharing the love and strength that lived in your heart.

> *Unless you can muse in a crowd all day*
> *In the absent face that fixed you;*
> *Unless you can love, as the angels may,*
> *With the breadth of heaven betwixt you;*
> *Unless you can dream that his faith is fast,*
> *Through behoving and unbehoving;*
> *Unless you can die when the dream is past —*
> *Oh, never call it loving!*

> *God answers sharp and sudden on some prayers,*
> *And thrusts the thing we have prayed for in our face,*
> *A gauntlet with a gift in 't.*

Henry Wadsworth Longfellow
1807-1882

M r. Longfellow has been written about and represented as a preacher of verse probably more than any other poet. He was a storyteller whose work had a sing-song meter and rhythm.

So on the ocean of life we pass and speak one another,
Only a look and a voice; then darkness again and a silence.

~

A boy's will is the wind's will,
And the thoughts of youth are long, long thoughts.

~

Read from some humbler poet,
Whose songs gushed from his heart,
As showers from the clouds of summer,
Or tears from the eyelids start.
Then read from the treasured volume
The poem of thy choice,
And lend to the rhyme of the poet
The beauty of thy voice.

~

And the night shall be filled with music,
And the cares, that infest the day,
Shall fold their tents, like the Arabs,
And as silently steal away.

~

Life is real! Life is earnest!
And the grave is not its goal;
Dust thou art, to dust returnest
Was not spoken of the soul.

His name is familiar as a poet whose works school children had to memorize.

Lives of great men all remind us
We can make our lives sublime,
And, departing, leave behind us
Footprints on the sands of time.

~

Let us, then, be up and doing,
With a heart for any fate;
Still achieving, still pursuing,
Learn to labour and to wait.

Sadly though, in the twentieth century, Mr. Longfellow's work has been less appreciated, and yet his words are felt and needed as much now as they were then.

A Lady with a Lamp shall stand
In the great history of the land,
A noble type of good,
Heroic womanhood.

He was a great scholar who traveled abroad when he was young,
and when he returned to America brought with him all the
romance he had absorbed in his journeys.

Silently one by one, in the infinite meadows of heaven
Blossomed the lovely stars, the forget-me-nots of the angels.

~

And the beauty and mystery of the ships,
And the music of the sea.

~

Music is the universal language of Mankind;
Poetry their universal pastime and delight.

~

The holiest of all holidays are those
Kept by ourselves in silence and apart;
The secret anniversaries of the heart.

~

How can I tell the signals and the signs
By which one heart another heart divines?
How can I tell the many thousand ways
By which it keeps the secret it betrays?

~

She floats upon the river of his thoughts.

Many of his works told stories that have become classics, like "Paul Revere's Ride," and seemed more ballad-like than poetry.

Look not mournfully into the Past.
It comes not back again. Wisely improve the Present.
It is thine. Go forth to meet the shadowy Future,
Without fear, and with a manly heart.

~

Out of the shadows of night
the world rolls into light;
It is daybreak everywhere.

~

Talk not of wasted affection! Affection never was wasted;
If it enrich not the heart of another, its waters returning
Back to their springs, like the rain, shall fill them full of refreshment.
That which the fountain sends forth returns again to the fountain.

~

If we could read the secret history of our enemies, we should find in
each man's life, sorrow and suffering enough to disarm all hostility.

~

A gentle boy, with soft and silken locks,
A dreamy boy, with brown and tender eyes,
A castle builder, with his wooden blocks
and towers that touch imaginary skies.

A fearless rider on his father's knee,
An eager listener unto stories told
At the Round Table of the nursery.
Of Heroes and adventures manifold.

There will be other towers for thee to build
There will be other steeds for thee to ride;
There will be other legends, and all filled
With greater marvels and more glorified.

Build on, and make thy castles high and fair,
Rising and reaching to the skies
Listen to voices in the upper air,
Nor lose thy simple faith and mystery.

Mr. Longfellow's first wife died in childbirth, and thirty years later his second wife died following an accident. After her death, he continued to write, but he never quite recovered from the shock of losing her.

Be still, sad heart! And cease repining;
Behind the clouds is the sun still shining.

~

There are things of which I may not speak
There are dreams that cannot die;
There are thoughts that make the strong heart weak,
Bring a pallor into the cheek and a mist before the eye.

His own death was mourned deeply in England and in America, and all the world lost one of its greatest poets. In memoriam, a marble image of Mr. Longfellow can be seen in The Poets' Corner in Westminster Abbey.

Time has laid his hand
Upon my heart, gently, not smiting it,
But as a harper lays his open palm
Upon his harp to deaden its vibrations.

~

Ye are better than all the ballads
That ever were sung or said;
For ye are loving poems,
And all the rest are dead.

~

No one is so accursed by fate,
No one so utterly desolate,
But some heart, though unknown,
Responds unto his own.

~

And with joy that is almost pain,
My heart goes back to wander there,
And among the dreams of the days that were
I find my lost youth again.

~

Give what you have. To someone, it may be better
than you dare to think.

And with this, dear sir, I close your chapter. This last stanza expresses such feeling in its simplicity that its visual beauty and love bring tears to my eyes.

> *And the boy who walked beside me,*
> *He could not understand*
> *Why closer in mine, ah closer,*
> *I pressed his warm, soft hand.*

JOHN GREENLEAF WHITTIER
1807-1892

○Mr. Whittier was born into a poor family. He lived his first eighteen years on a farm in New England. His first poem was published when he was nineteen.

> *The Night is mother of the Day*
> *The Winter of the Spring,*
> *And ever upon old Decay,*
> *The greenest mosses cling.*

> *Heap high the farmer's wintry hoard!*
> *Heap high the golden corn!*
> *No richer gift has autumn poured*
> *From out her lavish horn!*

> *Search thine own heart. What paineth thee*
> *In others in thyself may be.*

Because of his poverty, he had very little education, and was able to attend school for only a short time. Surely not an advantageous beginning for a poet, but perhaps this meager beginning gave this man the insight he needed to express himself. It certainly gave him determination, for he worked as a shoemaker and every penny he earned was spent on tuition for his two semesters of schooling.

> *God's ways seem dark, but soon or late,*
> *They touch the shining hills of day.*

> *If woman lost us Eden, such as she alone restore it.*

> *The tissue of the Life to be*
> *We weave with colors all our own,*
> *And in the field of Destiny*
> *We reap as we have sown.*

> *The windows of my soul ... I throw open to the sun.*

Most of Mr. Whittier's poems were written with a homespun flavor — simple poems reflecting his childhood. However, during one period, he became an adamantly militant poet who poured out his feelings into his work. He had no compulsions about the entire world knowing how he felt about slavery. His poetry became a one-man crusade to abolish the institution of slavery. Some, like "Barbara Frietchie" and "Skipper Ireson's Ride," along with "Snow-Bound," have become classics. To me, he is remembered largely as a poet whose words characterize the country farmboy living within him.

> *For of all sad words of tongue or pen*
> *The saddest are these, "It might have been!"*

No longer forward nor behind I look in hope or fear;
But, grateful, take the good I find, the best of now and here.

How little I have gained,
How vast the unattained.

Sweeter than any sung
My songs that found no tongue;
Nobler than any fact
My wish that failed of act.

He wrote countless volumes, and in his forties he began living in seclusion with his sister, just as Mr. Wordsworth had, continuing to write until he died at the age of eighty-five.

Flowers spring to blossom where she walks
The careful ways of duty;
Our hard, still lines of life with her
Are flowing curves of beauty.

Love watches o'er my quiet ways,
Kind voices speak my name
And lips that find it hard to praise
Are slow, at least, to blame.

God is and all is well.

With the sunshine on thy face,
Through thy torn brim's jaunty grace;
From my heart I give thee joy,
I was once a barefoot boy!

Oh for boyhood's time of June,
Crowding years in one brief moon,
When all the things I heard or saw,
Me, their master waited for.

I was rich in flowers and tears,
Humming birds and honey bees ...
Ah! That thou could know thy joy.
'Ere it passes, barefoot boy!

How thrills once more the lengthening
Chain of memory at the thought of thee!
Old hopes which long in dust have lain,
Old dreams, come thronging back again,
And boyhood lives again in me.

For more to me than birds or flowers,
My playmate left her home,
And took with her the laughing spring,
The music and the bloom.

Mr. Whittier's works have a story-telling quality and a simplicity
that reaches me with a kindred tenderness. I first read

"School Days" when I was ten. Remembering my admiration for this poet, who could capture so visually his feelings in this simple story of truth and childhood love, I chose a stanza from it to illustrate one of my paintings selected for reproduction in the 1960s.

Later with more confidence, my own words and art began flowing together comfortably and easily into my artwork, and I realized I was combining both painting and poetry. This major change brought my career into a broader and more identifiable direction, and led me into the world of writing that I had so loved yet always considered to be separate from my art. The following is Mr. Whittier's "School Days."

Still sits the school-house by the road,
A ragged beggar sleeping;
Around it still the sumachs grow
And blackberry-vines are creeping.
Within, the master's desk is seen,
Deep scarred by raps official;
The warping floor, the battered seats,
The Jack-knife's carved initial;

Long years ago a winter sun
Shone over it at setting;
Lit up its western window-panes,
And low eaves' icy fretting.

It touched the tangled golden curls,
And brown eyes full of grieving,
Of one who still her step delayed
When all the school were leaving.

For near her stood the little boy
Her childish favor singled;
His cap pulled low upon a face
Where pride and shame were mingled.

Pushing with restless feet the snow
To right and left, he lingered; …
As restlessly her tiny hands
The blue-checked apron fingered.

He saw her lift her eyes; he felt
The soft hand's light caressing,
And heard the tremble of her voice,
As if a fault confessing.

'I'm sorry that I spelt the word:
I hate to go above you,
Because,' … the brown eyes lower fell, …
'Because, you see, I love you!'

Still memory to a gray-haired man
That sweet child-face is showing.
Dear girl! The grasses on her grave
Have forty years been growing!

He lives to learn, in life's hard school,
How few who pass above him,
Lament their triumph and his loss
Like her, … because they love him.

Thank you, Mr. Whittier.

ALFRED, LORD TENNYSON
1809-1892

*A*lfred Tennyson was born in the Lincolnshire village of
Somersby, one of eleven children. He was raised in comfort,
his childhood filled with a tranquility often reflected in his
work. As a boy he was fascinated by stories of King Arthur,
which grew into a lifelong interest. He was acclaimed by many
to be one of the greatest poets of his generation, or perhaps of
his century.

> *If time be heavy on your hands,*
> *Are there no beggars at your gate,*
> *Nor any poor about your lands?*
> *Oh! Teach the orphan-boy to read,*
> *Or teach the orphan-girl to sew.*
>
> ~
>
> *Here at the quiet limit of the world.*
>
> ~
>
> *We are not cotton-spinners all.*
>
> ~
>
> *Once in a golden hour, I cast to earth a seed.*
> *Up there came a flower, the people said a weed.*

Our hoard is little but our hearts are great.

Like glimpses of forgotten dreams.

Music that gentler on the spirit lies,
Than tir'd eyelids upon tir'd eyes;
Music that brings sweet sleep down
From the blissful skies.

Like so many others, he began writing when he was very young.
At fourteen his work showed his deep feelings for English
Renaissance poetry, and by eighteen, he and his brother wrote
and published their first volume.

The useful trouble of the rain.

A simple maiden in her flower
Is worth a hundred coats of arms.

In the spring a young man's fancy lightly turns
to thoughts of love.

Let us alone. Time driveth onward fast,
And in a little while our lips are dumb.
Let us alone. What is that will last?

All things are taken from us, and become
Portions and parcels of the dreadful Past.

~

God gives us love. Something to love
He lends us; but when love is grown
To ripeness, that on which it grows
Falls off, and love is left alone.

~

Like a dog, he hunts in dreams.

~

He will hold thee when his passion shall have
spent its novel force,
Something better than his dog, a little dearer
than his horse.

He attended Cambridge and became close friends with a group
including Edward Fitzgerald and a friend named Arthur Henry
Hallam, who later died at the age of twenty-two. Mr. Tennyson
was so strongly affected by his friend's death that he became ill.
His grief was so deep that he wrote much about his kindred
friend, Mr. Hallam.

Never morning wore to evening, but some heart did break.

~

Thrice blest whose lives are faithful prayers,
Whose loves in higher love endure;
What souls posses themselves so pure,
Or is there blessedness like theirs?

~

Short swallow-flights of song, that dip
Their wings in tears, and skim away.

~

The sweetest soul that ever look'd with human eyes.

~

I sometimes hold it half a sin
To put in words the grief I feel;
For words, like Nature, half reveal
And half conceal the Soul within.

~

But O for the touch of a vanish'd hand,
And the sound of a voice that is still.

~

He seems so near, and yet so far.

~

Weaving all that weight
Of learning lightly like a flower.

For many years he went into semi-seclusion and was even reluctant to meet Mr. Wordsworth who had requested a meeting. But they did meet, and afterwards Mr. Wordsworth was so impressed with him and his work that he bestowed a pension upon him, and called him the "the first of our living poets."

In after dinner talk,
Across the walnuts and the wine.

~

Sleep sweetly, tender heart, in pearl;
Sleep, holy spirit, blessed soul,
While the stars burn, the moons increase,
And the great ages onward roll.

~

Tears, idle tears, I know not what they mean,
Tears from the depth of some divine despair
Rise in the heart, and gather to the eyes,
In looking on the happy autumn fields,
And thinking of the days that are no more.

~

But the tender grace of a day that is dead,
will never come back to me.

At forty-one he married, and their first child was named
Hallam, after his friend. Often, Mr. Tennyson's work combined
romance with a touch of morality.

The old order changeth, yielding place to new;
And God fulfills himself in many ways,
Lest one good custom should corrupt the world.

~

More things are wrought by prayer
Than this world dreams of. Wherefore, let thy voice
Rise like a fountain for me night and day.

Be near me when my light is low.

Behold, we know not anything;
I can trust that good shall fall
At last ... far off ... at last, to all,
And every winter change to spring.

Knowledge comes, but wisdom lingers.

Where we fall out with those we love
and kiss again with tears!

Dear as remembered kisses after death,
And sweet as those by hopeless fancy feign'd
On lips that are for others; deep as love,
Deep as first love, and wild with all regret;
O Death in Life, the days that are no more.

There is sweet music here that softer falls
Than petals from blown roses on the grass.

As this was the early Victorian age, the moralizing that Mr. Tennyson showed in his work seemed quite natural for a poet who thought as deeply as he did. He wrote plays and often read before the Queen, who, like many others, found a minstrel quality to his work. He was ultimately knighted for his work as a poet, and became Alfred, Lord Tennyson.

> *He gave the people of his best;*
> *His worst he kept, his best he gave.*

Lord Tennyson, having such admiration for the beauty in the melancholy of your work, and the skill with which you write, makes it difficult for me to select a verse to end this chapter. I quite understand why you remained England's most popular poet until your death in 1892.

> *And in her lover's arm she leant,*
> *And round her waist she felt it fold,*
> *And far across the hills they went*
> *On that new world which is the old.*

> ~

> *To love one maiden only, cleave to her*
> *And worship her by years of golden deeds.*

> ~

> *And quoted odes, and jewels five-words-long*
> *That on the stretched forefinger of all time*
> *Sparkle forever.*

> ~

> *For why is all around us here*
> *As if some lesser god had made the world,*
> *But had not force to shape it as he would?*

For the lyrical beauty and minstrel quality I feel in your work, dear sir, I close your chapter, with my gratitude.

To where beyond these voices there is peace.

~

Flower in the crannied wall
I pluck you out of the crannies,
I hold you here, root and all, in my hand,
Little flower — but if I could understand
What you are, root and all, and all in all,
I should know what God and man is.

~

O Swallow, Swallow, flying, flying South,
Fly to her, and fall upon her gilded eaves,
And tell her, tell her, what I tell to Thee.

~

I found Him in the shining of the stars,
I mark'd Him in the flowering of His fields,
But in His way with men I find Him not.

~

For who loves me must have a touch of earth …

~

In me there dwells no greatness, save it be some far-off
touch of greatness to know well I am not great.

Robert Browning
1812-1889

$\mathscr{B}$orn in London, Mr. Browning never attended a university, but was educated by his mother and father. His father was such a lover of the classics, it is said he possessed an unbelievable seven thousand books in his library. His son's career was directed and planned for while he was still very young.

> In the morning of the world,
> When earth was nigher heaven than now.

> ~

> The year's at the spring and day's at the morn;
> Morning's at seven; the hillside's dew-pearled;
> The lark's on the wing; the snail's on the thorn:
> God's in his heaven — all's right with the world.

His first collection of verses was published at the age of twelve, but he later destroyed them. He traveled a great deal in his twenties and became enchanted with Italy. He was involved with writing dramas for a time, then went back to poetry.

> Measure your mind's height by the shade it casts!

~

Round the cape of a sudden came the sea,
And the sun looked over the mountain's rim:
And straight was a path of gold for him,
And the need of a world of men for me.

~

And had you only heard me play one time, or viewed me
from a window, not so soon with you ... would such things fade as
with the rest.

His entire life was dedicated to his writing, and he wrote
constantly. Other poets influenced him, Shelley being the one
whose work he admired the most, but Mr. Browning seemed to
be determined to write in his own style. His romance with
Elizabeth Barrett began by a letter of thanks to her in response
to one of her poems in which she had praised him. The praise
turned into love and they were married.

Teach me, only teach, Love!
As I ought
I will speak thy speech, Love,
Think thy thought.

~

God be thanked, the meanest of his creatures
Boasts two soul-sides, one to face the world with,
One to show a woman when he loves her!

His life had been so different from Elizabeth's. His father was warm and sympathetic, and hers was jealous and domineering. It is no wonder theirs was a love story that will live forever in history, like their poetry. Mr. Browning's career didn't reach its height until he was forty-four years old. No other poet who had ever lived, with the exception of Mr. Shakespeare, had written poetry that completely described the human spirit in its entirety.

All that I know
Of a certain star
Is, it can throw
(Like the angled spar)
Now a dart of red,
Now a dart of blue;
Till my friends have said
They would fain see, too,
My star that dartles the red and the blue!
Then it stops like a bird; like a flower, hangs furled:
They must solace themselves with the Saturn above it,
What matter to me if their star is a world?
Mine has opened its soul to me; therefore I love it.

~

Thoughts may be over-poetical for poetry.

~

Never the time and the place
And the loved one all together!

~

Look not down, but up!

~

This could but have happened once —
And we missed it, lost it forever.

~

Stung by the splendour of a sudden thought.

~

You never know what life means till you die:
Even throughout life, 'tis death that makes life live.
Gives it whatever the significance.

~

We find great things are made of little things,
And little things go lessening till at last
Comes God behind them.

Mr. Browning's poems had characters like dramas, yet he was unsuccessful as a dramatist, and found his place in poetry.

This is a spray the bird clung to,
making it blossom with pleasure.

~

Ah, but a man's reach should exceed his grasp,
or what's a heaven for?

~

How good is man's life, the mere living! How fit to employ
All the heart and the soul and the senses forever in joy!

After his wife died, he left Italy for England, never returning to the city where they had found such happiness.

Oh, the little more, and how much it is!
And the little less, and what worlds away!

~

She had a heart — how shall I say? —
too soon made glad.

~

Only I discern infinite passion,
and the pain of finite hearts that yearn.

~

Earth being so good, would heaven seem best?

~

So hush … I will give you this leaf to keep …
See, I shut it inside the sweet cold hand.
There, that is our secret: go to sleep!
You will wake, and remember, and understand.

The last years of his life brought many honors. He was persistent in striving for perfection. He believed that everything could be ideal, and if one could keep on searching, it would almost become a creed for mankind. Mr. Browning, what joy you and your Elizabeth must have had. It would have been enough to have shared such a love, but to share the joys of each other's work must have been the secret that made the music flow so beautifully from you both. I believe only joy or sadness can make the creative mind express the true feelings of the human heart … and I thank you, for all that your heart has given me. As your chapter ends, I choose some of your writings that express my own feelings.

I have lived, seen God's hand through a lifetime,
And all was for best.

~

What I aspired to be,
And was not, comforts me.

~

What I call God,
And fools call Nature.

~

Grow old along with me!
The best is yet to be,
The last of life, for which the first was made:
Our times are in his hand.
Who saith: 'A whole I planned,
Youth shows itself but half; trust God, see all, nor be afraid.'

~

Would you have your songs endure?
Build on the human heart.

~

There is but one way to browbeat this world,
Dumb-founder doubt, and repay scorn in kind, ...
To go on trusting, namely, till faith moves mountains.

~

Have you found your life distasteful?
My life did and does smack sweet.
Was your youth of pleasure wasteful?
Mine I saved and hold complete.
Do your joys with age diminish?
When mine fail me, I'll complain.
Must in death your daylight finish?
My sun sets to rise again.

~

The great mind knows the power of gentleness,
Only tries force, because persuasion fails.

JAMES RUSSELL LOWELL
1819-1891

Mr. Lowell was born in Cambridge, Massachusetts, and educated at Harvard. While attending school there, he changed his plans from law to literature. He married a girl who was an abolitionist and liberal and who became a great influence upon him. His poems published from 1844 through 1867 brought him great notice both as a romantic poet and as a critic.

All thoughts that mould the age begin
Deep down within the primitive soul.

Dear common flower, that grow'st beside the way,
Fringing the dusty road with harmless gold.

And what is so rare as a day in June?
Then if ever, come perfect days;
Then Heaven tries the earth if it be in tune,
And over it softly her warm ear lays.

Each year to ancient friendships adds a ring,
As to an oak.

She doeth little kindnesses
which most leave undone, or despise.

~

Not only around our infancy
doth heaven with all its splendors lie;
Daily, with souls that cringe and plot,
We Sinais climb and know it not.

Some political poems also established Mr. Lowell as a satirist, showing his great wit, as well as his talent.

The gift without the giver is bare;
Who gives himself with his alms feeds three,
Himself, his hungering neighbor and me.

~

Folks never understand the folks they hate.

After his wife died, he became professor of modern languages at Harvard for more then twenty years. He also became editor of the *Atlantic Monthly* and the *American Review*, both literary publications.

It is by presence of mind in untried emergencies
that the native metal of a man is tested.

~

'Tis heaven alone that is given away;
'Tis only God may be had for the asking.

~

Be noble! And the nobleness that lies
In other men, sleeping, but never dead,
Will rise in majesty to meet thine own.

~

Great truths are portions of the soul of man;
Great souls are portions of Eternity.

~

A weed is no more than a flower in disguise,
which is seen through at once, if love give a man eyes.

After the Civil War, Mr. Lowell turned more towards scholarship and also became a critic.

His words were simple words enough,
And yet he used them so,
That what in other mouths was rough,
In his seemed musical and low.

~

He gives only the worthless gold
who gives from a sense of duty.

~

Nature fits all her children with something to do,
He who would write and can't write, can surely review.

He was appointed Minister to Madrid, and later Minister to London, where he stayed for almost ten years. During this time in his life, he did much to bring about respect for American letters and institutions.

What a sense of security in an old
book which Time has criticized for us!

In life's small things be resolute and great
To keep thy muscle trained; know'st thou when Fate
Thy measure takes, or when she'll say to thee,
"I find thee worthy; do this deed for me?"

The nurse of full-grown souls is solitude.

The wisest man could ask no more of Fate
Than to be simple, modest, manly, true,
Safe from the Many, honored by the Few;
To count as naught in World, or Church, or State;
But inwardly in secret to be great.

No man is born into the world whose work
Is not born with him; there is always work,
And tools to work withal, for those who will;
And blessed are the horny hands of toil.

Safe is the hallowed quiet of the past.

Solitude is as needful to the imagination
as society is wholesome for the character.

Dear Mr. Lowell, I feel the tenderness of human emotion floating ever so through your work. I end your chapter with chosen thoughts you've expressed, each one important to me.

When I was a beggarly boy,
And lived in a cellar damp,
I had not a friend nor a toy,
But I had Aladdin's lamp.

Every man feels instinctively that all the beautiful
sentiments in the world
Weigh less than a simple lovely action.

Things always seem fairer when we look back at them,
and it is out of that inaccessible tower of the past, that
longing leans and beckons.

She is a woman; one in whom
The springtime of her childish years
Hath never lost its fresh perfume,
though knowing well
That life hath room for many blights
and many tears.

To All The Poets

The writing of this book is a labor of love, and in a way closes a chapter in my life.

It's late. The darkest blue of night is almost here, as I write in my upstairs studio. I watch two sparrows as they flutter near the outside window ledge near me. It is cold, and I find myself wishing I could let them inside.

With moonlight floating across the room, I notice an old wooden box on my desk, and a child's handprint in clay hanging on the wall above it. The deeply carved initials show plainly their childlike crookedness in this light, and the handprint shows accidental indentations left by a proud five-year-old. Suddenly I am wrapped in a warm, deep feeling of love, and silently give thanks for being alive.

And now I must end this letter and also this time with you. I thank you once more, collectively, for enriching my life.

Along with my uncle, Jack, you inspire me still as you continue to feed the passion I feel for the romance of this sweet life. I will always be grateful — and hope you know that it is because of you my heart sings.

Goodnight, my friends.
November 19, 1973

Flavia Weedn

Flavia Weedn

Flavia Weedn is one of America's leading inspirational writers and illustrators. The core of her life's work consists of encouraging the expression of real feelings and bringing hope to the human spirit. Over the past four decades, Flavia has touched the lives of millions through books, cards, fine stationery products, posters and hundreds of licensed goods available throughout the world.

Flavia lives and works in Santa Barbara, California, where she has just completed her autobiography.

A few can touch the magic string,

And noisy Fame is proud to win them;

Alas for those that never sing,

But die with all their music in them!

— *Oliver Wendell Holmes*